D0667681

May these wonderful words and special insights provide you with encouragement and joy… and may they help to inspire your life!

ISBN: 978-1-59842-906-0

◪ and Blue Mountain Press are registered in U.S. Patent and Trademark Office. Certain trademarks are used under license.

Printed in China.
Fourth Printing: 2019

✪ This book is printed on recycled paper.

This book is printed on paper that has been specially produced to be acid free (neutral pH) and contains no groundwood or unbleached pulp. It conforms with the requirements of the American National Standards Institute, Inc., so as to ensure that this book will last and be enjoyed by future generations.

Blue Mountain Arts, Inc.
P.O. Box 4549, Boulder, Colorado 80306

Make Every Day a Positive One

A book of encouragement, hope, and great advice

Douglas Pagels

Blue Mountain Press™

Boulder, Colorado

About the Author

Best-selling author and editor Douglas Pagels has inspired millions of readers with his insights and his anthologies. His books have sold over 3 million copies, and he is one of the most quoted contemporary writers on the Internet today. Reflecting a philosophy that is perfect for our times, Doug has a wonderful  knack for sharing his thoughts and sentiments in a voice that is so positive and understanding we can't help but take the message to heart.

His writings have been translated into over a dozen languages due to their global appeal and inspiring outlook on life, and his work has been quoted by many worthy causes and charitable organizations.

He and his wife live in Colorado, and they are both parents and grandparents. Over the years, Doug has spent much of his time as a classroom volunteer, a youth basketball coach, an advocate for local environmental issues, a frequent traveler, and a craftsman, building a cabin in the Rocky Mountains.

*B*e optimistic about as many things as possible, realistic about things requiring an exact, matter-of-fact outlook, and pessimistic… about absolutely nothing at all.

*M*ake yourself available.
Make a difference.
And make your days just shine.

*Y*ou deserve all the happiness in the world. And gradually, over the course of your life… I hope that's exactly what you find.

Stay motivated.
Never stop wondering, wandering, and imagining. Curiosity, creativity, fulfillment, and achievement all go hand in hand, and they're good travel companions to have along on your journey.

More things are possible in your life than you can possibly imagine.

*A*s a wise man once said, "Just press on." That's how you get almost everything — power buttons, lights, and life — to work.

My advice to you: No matter what happens, remember... the music is always going to change... and a different dance is better than no dance at all. Being able to adapt to the moment, think on your feet, and partner up with what's possible will someday have you kicking up your heels as you head off in a happier direction.

*I*n the dance of life, most people consider moving forward as the only way to go. I guess that's why we're all so flustered when something happens to change the tune… and we're confronted with having to perform a little improvised do-si-do.

*S*uggestions and directions for the road ahead...

Try to keep your distance from people whose middle names could literally be "It's All About Me." Never grow apart from friends, even if they're far away. And always try to get closer to those breath-of-fresh-air people who brighten up your life... people who are warm-hearted, understanding, and uplifting and who listen closely and care about the answer you give when they ask how you are.

*L*ife is short.
Do what you long for, do what you love, and
begin doing it... now.

*L*et's all agree on this: In order to
meet your daily needs and responsibilities,
you have to listen to what your head is
telling you. But how you spend your free
time? That should be a reflection of what
your heart is yearning to do.

Do things that are a reflection of your feelings toward others.

Do what makes you feel good about your place in the world. Do things that make you smile and things that bring you hope and things that open doors.

Use your time and energy to help so many blessings come to you... and yours.

*Y*ou only have so much time and energy.

It's your call, but if I were you, I would pretty much put those hours and efforts into the things that matter most. Do what provides you with a nice sense of security and inner peace.

Do what makes you proud of what you've done.

*B*e efficient.

Efficient people do things just as well as procrastinators — they just do them faster. The more you can streamline the methodical "move this from column A to column B" parts of your life, the more time you'll have for the juicy, enjoyable, rewarding parts of your life.

One great decision made at one special time in your life can lead to everything after being better and shining brighter.

That person who was such a gem is just as priceless and as precious right now. Your life experiences are richer, your relationships are deeper, and many things are so much sweeter. As we age, we are supposed to become wiser.

And one of the smartest things anyone can do is appreciate who you are, what you are, and where you are... so gratefully today.

*W*e always hear the adage that we shouldn't compare ourselves with others.

But this is true too: don't compare who you are today… with the younger you. It's easy to imagine what you looked like then… and what you could do that you may not do so gracefully today.

And you should remind yourself that the more of those periods you put in, the farther you'll be from that awkward beginning... and the closer you'll be to a marvelous end.

*T*hat project you need to complete or that goal you want to meet?

Start... by getting started. Today. No more delays. Just remind yourself that you can do almost anything for half an hour... and this job is what you're going to do. Then, after those thirty minutes are up, take a deep breath and give yourself a few moments to review, reflect, and reassess. You can then continue on, whenever the time is right, thirty minutes at a time, for as long as it takes.

*W*hen you stroll along and unwind outside under a great big beautiful sky, you can actually walk your worries away.

*G*o in search of nature's special places. The wilder, the better. Sit down and listen. Spend time there and learn. Return from your adventure and remember. And don't wait too long to go back again.

*I*f the bluebird of happiness hasn't landed on your shoulder in a while, maybe you need to consider putting on your walking shoes and wandering over to where bluebirds abound.

It seems like I see a lot of them wherever people are active, eating right, staying fit, and maintaining the highest level of health they can.

Is it true that the healthier you are, the happier you can be? Absolutely.

I have some good news about your future.

Yesterday is behind you. What's done is done, and it's important for you to take what you've learned from the past and just move on. Today is a brand-new opportunity, a blank canvas, an unwritten page... just waiting to see. All that needs to happen right now is for you to do all the amazing things you're capable of...

And tomorrow? That's the place where promises come true. You'll need to be smart and stay strong to live the life you want to have. But don't ever forget: you are creative and capable and wise, and I know you have what it takes to make your days everything you want them to be. And remember this for sure...

You can't change a single thing about the past, but you can change absolutely everything about the future.

*F*ill in the blank:
I'm so lucky to be _____ .

Then... with that phrase in mind, fill up your heart... and smile accordingly.

*W*hen your heart is filled with gratitude for what you do have, your head isn't nearly so worried about what you don't.

*S*ometimes it's important to work for that pot of gold. But other times it's essential to take time off and to make sure that your most important decision in the day simply consists of choosing which color to slide down on the rainbow.

May You Be Blessed with All These Things

A little more joy, a little less stress,
a lot more recognition of your wonderfulness.

Abundance in your life, blessings in your days,
dreams that come true, and hopes that stay.

A rainbow on the horizon, an angel by your side,
and everything that could ever bring
a smile to your life.

*D*on't simply exist.
Flourish.

*B*e authentic.
Genuine. Honest. Sincere. Flaws and all.
Assets galore. Don't pretend to be someone
else. Just be you. Amazing, one-of-a-kind,
remarkable, refreshing, what-a-blessing-to-
have-you-here… you!

*D*o what rivers do. They flow on and move forward, gathering strength along the way. And they occasionally have turbulent times to deal with, but they always — always — find a way to get where they're going.

*M*ake choices you — and the person you will be ten years from now — will be happy with.

A good way to help you decide on a course of action involves answering these two questions:
What will I gain if I do this?
What will I lose if I don't?

*D*on't be passive when you need to be active. Don't just imagine yourself living more fully. If you want to change and be a better you, it's time to turn off those old excuses and embrace new possibilities. Do what will make the "future you" so happy about the love you've decided to show yourself and the wonderful plan you've put in place. Be a person who makes a point of living more fully and who — when waking up in the morning — has a lot more smiles to greet the day.

*W*henever you get to a turning point in your life, think of it as a chance to turn into more of the person you want to be.

*S*et an intention.
What do you want to accomplish in the weeks and months and years ahead? Write your intention down and tape it to a mirror where you'll see it every day. Use it as a loving reminder of where you're headed and why you're going in that direction.

And then, when you see the reflection of a wonderful person smiling back at you, you'll also see who you're making happy as the goal gets closer and closer to being met.

There's an old saying that goes like this...

"I'd rather have a life of oh-wells than a life of what-ifs."

— Author Unknown

I wish so many wonderful things for you. I want your present moments to be filled with so much happiness!

I think that some of the best gifts we can receive are the ones we get when we really embrace life — and put our whole heart into it. They say that you get in life what you have the courage to ask for. When it comes to anything — whether it involves people or places or jobs or hoped-for plans — you never know what the answer will be if you don't ask.

And you never know what the result will be if you don't try.

May you always keep the faith, continue to work to make things better, get up after you've been knocked down, and remember that each tomorrow is a new day. Make good choices, connect with great people, and never forget that the best things of all are often just around the corner.

I want you to be rewarded with all the smiles life could ever give to anyone...
     and have every blessing you deserve
          in all the days to come.

*H*ave faith.

There are things in life you'll have to overcome. Faith keeps you from going overboard with worry and frustration and doubt. You <u>will</u> manage, and the more faith you have, the less energy you'll waste on the wrong things. You'll right the ship and sail on. And when the next difficulty comes along, the "older and wiser" you will be very capable of dealing with that one too.